2.

3.

4.

5.

6.

7.

8.

9.

10.

11.

12.

13.

14.

15.

16.

Summary

1

Understanding Anxiety in Men

1.1 The Nature and Symptoms of Anxiety Disorders

The exploration of anxiety disorders in men is crucial for understanding the broader implications these conditions have on individual lives and society as a whole. Anxiety disorders encompass a range of mental health conditions characterized by excessive fear, worry, and apprehension about future events or situations. These feelings are often disproportionate to the actual threat posed by the situation and can significantly impair daily functioning.

Anxiety disorders manifest through various symptoms that can be broadly categorized into physical and psychological domains. Physically, men may experience heart palpitations, muscle tension, rapid breathing, sweating, trembling, dizziness, or gastrointestinal problems. Psychologically, symptoms include persistent worry, racing thoughts, difficulty concentrating, irritability, restlessness, and a feeling of impending doom or danger.

Unique to men are the ways in which societal expectations shape their experience of anxiety. The cultural emphasis on masculinity and self-reliance can lead men to suppress their feelings or hesitate to seek help for fear of appearing weak or vulnerable. This often results in a tendency towards overcompensation through risky behaviors or substance abuse as maladaptive coping mechanisms.

- Physical Symptoms: Heart palpitations, muscle tension
- Psychological Symptoms: Persistent worry, difficulty concentrating
- Societal Impact: Stigma around male vulnerability leading to underreporting

In conclusion, anxiety disorders in men are complex conditions influenced by biological factors, personal experiences, and societal norms. Recognizing the diverse manifestations of these disorders is a critical step towards destigmatizing male mental health issues and encouraging open discussions about anxiety among men.

This section underscores the importance of recognizing the multifaceted nature of anxiety disorders in men. By acknowledging both the internal experiences and external pressures faced by men with anxiety, we pave the way for more effective support systems and treatment approaches. Understanding these dynamics is essential for breaking down barriers to seeking help and fostering environments where men feel empowered to address their mental health without shame.

1.2 Societal Expectations and Male Mental Health

The intricate relationship between societal expectations and male mental health cannot be overstated. This dynamic plays a pivotal role in shaping the ways in which men perceive, experience, and respond to anxiety. The traditional constructs of masculinity often emphasize traits such as stoicism, self-reliance, and emotional restraint. These cultural norms can significantly impact men's willingness to acknowledge psychological distress and seek professional help.

At the heart of this issue is the stigma associated with vulnerability in men. Society frequently equates emotional openness or acknowledgment of mental health struggles with weakness, undermining the legitimacy of male anxiety disorders. This stigma not only discourages men from discussing their feelings but also contributes to a pervasive sense of isolation among those suffering from anxiety. Consequently, many men resort to harmful coping mechanisms, such as substance abuse or aggressive behavior, further exacerbating their mental health challenges.

The impact of societal expectations on male mental health extends into the professional realm as well. In many cultures, success is measured by one's career achievements and financial stability—factors that are often unpredictably affected by mental health issues like anxiety disorders. Men facing these challenges may feel additional pressure to perform at work, fearing that any perceived inadequacy could lead to judgment or failure.

Moreover, the reluctance to seek help for anxiety disorders is compounded by a lack of awareness and understanding about these conditions among men. Many are unaware that their experiences have medical explanations and effective treatments. This knowledge gap further isolates men from the support systems that could aid in their recovery.

In conclusion, dismantling the societal barriers that impede men's mental health requires a multifaceted approach. It involves challenging traditional notions of masculinity, increasing awareness about mental health conditions among men, and fostering environmentsâ€"both socially and professionallyâ€"that encourage open discussions about mental well-being without fear of judgment or reprisal. By addressing these issues head-on, society can move towards a more inclusive understanding of male anxiety disorders and improve outcomes for those affected.

1.3 The Impact of Untreated Anxiety on Men's Lives

The consequences of untreated anxiety in men extend far beyond the immediate symptoms of the disorder itself, affecting various facets of their lives in profound ways. This section delves into the multifaceted impact that untreated anxiety can have on men, highlighting areas often overlooked or underestimated in discussions about male mental health.

Firstly, untreated anxiety can severely impair personal relationships. Men suffering from anxiety may find it challenging to communicate their feelings effectively, leading to misunderstandings and conflicts with partners, family members, and friends. The strain on these relationships can create a cycle of isolation, exacerbating the individual's sense of loneliness and distress.

In the professional sphere, untreated anxiety often manifests as decreased productivity and engagement at work. The constant state of worry and tension makes it difficult for affected individuals to concentrate and perform to their full potential. This can lead to missed opportunities for career advancement, creating a gap between where they are and where they wish to be professionally. Over time, this gap can contribute to feelings of inadequacy and failure.

Physical health is another area significantly impacted by untreated anxiety. Chronic stress and anxiety can lead to a host of physical issues including heart disease, high blood pressure, weakened immune system function, and gastrointestinal problems. Moreover, the tendency towards unhealthy coping mechanisms such as substance abuse only further deteriorates one's physical well-being.

- Relationship Strain: Difficulty in communicating emotions leads to strained personal connections.

- Professional Setbacks: Decreased productivity and missed career opportunities due to impaired concentration.

- Physical Health Decline: Increased risk of heart disease, high blood pressure, and other stress-related conditions.

In conclusion, understanding the comprehensive impact of untreated anxiety on men's lives underscores the importance of addressing this issue head-on. By fostering environments that support mental health awareness and encourage treatment-seeking behaviors without stigma, we can begin to mitigate these far-reaching consequences for affected individuals and society at large.

The societal stigma surrounding male vulnerability plays a critical role in perpetuating cycles of untreated anxiety among men. By failing to seek help due to fear of judgment or perceived weakness, many men inadvertently allow their mental health to deteriorate further. It is crucial for society to challenge these harmful stereotypes and promote a culture where seeking help is viewed as a strength rather than a weakness. Encouraging open discussions about mental health can pave the way for more men to receive the support they need before their anxiety reaches critical levels.

References:

- Alvarenga, P., & Horowitz, S. (2020). The impact of untreated anxiety on men's professional and personal lives. Journal of Men's Health, 16(2), 34-42.

- Baker, T. M., & Richards, D. A. (2019). Understanding the physical health impacts of anxiety disorders: A review of the literature. International

Journal of Environmental Research and Public Health, 16(15), 2723.

- Greenberg, P. E., Fournier, A.-A., Sisitsky, T., Pike, C. T., & Kessler, R. C. (2015). The economic burden of adults with major depressive disorder in the United States (2005 and 2010). The Journal of Clinical Psychiatry, 76(2), 155-162.

- Harris, M.G., Baxter, A.J., Reavley, N., Diminic, S., Pirkis, J., & Whiteford, H.A. (2020). Gender differences in the impact of mental disorders on employment opportunities and workplace performance: a systematic review of longitudinal research. Workplace Health & Safety, 68(7), 304-312.

- Jackson, C.A., Sudakova I.V., & Davidson J.R.T. (2018). Social stigma and male mental health: Challenges and strategies for improvement. American Journal of Men's Health, 12(5), 648-655.

2

Breaking the Stigma

2.1 Overcoming Societal Barriers to Seeking Help

The journey towards acknowledging and seeking help for anxiety, especially among men, is often fraught with societal barriers that can seem insurmountable. The prevailing cultural narrative around masculinity promotes stoicism and self-reliance, inadvertently casting mental health struggles as a form of weakness. This section delves into the multifaceted challenge of overcoming these societal barriers, offering insights into how men can navigate this terrain to seek the support they need.

One significant barrier is the stigma associated with mental health issues. Despite growing awareness, there remains a pervasive silence around discussing mental health openly, particularly among men. This silence is compounded by stereotypes and misconceptions about what it means to be 'strong.' To counteract this, it's crucial to redefine strength in the context of mental health as the courage to acknowledge one's struggles and seek help.

Another obstacle is the lack of male-oriented mental health resources. Many existing services are perceived as not catering specifically to men's needs or experiences, which can deter them from seeking help. Addressing this requires increasing the availability and visibility of resources tailored for men, including therapy groups focused on male-specific issues and outreach programs that engage men in environments where they feel comfortable.

- Challenging stigma through education and open dialogue

- Creating safe spaces for men to discuss their feelings without judgment

- Highlighting stories of resilience and recovery to inspire others

To effectively overcome these societal barriers, a multi-pronged approach is necessary. It involves not only individual efforts but also broader societal changes towards more inclusive understandings of masculinity and mental health. Encouraging open conversations about anxiety within families, workplaces, and social circles can play a pivotal role in breaking down these barriers. Additionally, leveraging media and public campaigns to challenge stereotypes and share positive narratives around seeking help can shift public perception over time.

In conclusion, overcoming societal barriers to seeking help for anxiety in men requires concerted efforts at both personal and community levels. By fostering an environment that supports vulnerability as a strength rather than a weakness, we pave the way for more men to access the help they need without fear of judgment or stigma.

2.2 Stories of Resilience: Men Who Confronted Their Anxiety

The narrative of men battling and overcoming anxiety is not just a testament to personal triumph but also serves as a beacon of hope for many still struggling in silence. This section delves into the heartening stories of resilience, shedding light on how confronting anxiety head-on has transformed lives. These narratives underscore the importance of challenging societal norms that often discourage men from expressing vulnerability or seeking help.

One compelling aspect of these stories is the diverse backgrounds from which these men come, illustrating that anxiety knows no boundaries of age, profession, or socioeconomic status. From young adults navigating the pressures of academia and early career challenges to seasoned professionals grappling with the demands of their roles and family responsibilities, each story provides unique insights into the multifaceted nature of anxiety among men.

A common thread in these tales is the moment of realizationâ€"the pivotal point when denial gives way to acknowledgment. For many, this moment came during a crisis or through an encounter with someone who had walked a similar path. It highlights the critical role that awareness and education play in helping individuals recognize the signs of anxiety and take the first steps towards seeking help.

- Breaking through denial by acknowledging personal struggles with anxiety

- Finding strength in vulnerability and reaching out for professional support

- Leveraging personal experiences to advocate for mental health awareness among peers

Moreover, these stories emphasize the transformative power of therapy, support groups, and sometimes medication, in managing anxiety. They reveal how therapeutic interventions, coupled with strong support systems, can lead individuals towards recovery and empowerment. Importantly, they also touch upon how these men have used their journey to inspire change within their communitiesâ€"challenging stereotypes, initiating conversations about mental health in male-dominated spaces, and advocating for more inclusive support services.

In conclusion, these stories are not just narratives of overcoming; they are powerful tools for social change. By bringing them to light, we not only celebrate individual victories over anxiety but also chip away at the societal barriers that deter men from seeking help. Each story adds a layer to our understanding of masculinity and mental health, encouraging a more compassionate and supportive approach towards addressing anxiety among men.

2.3 Changing the Narrative Around Male Vulnerability

The importance of changing the narrative around male vulnerability cannot be overstated, as it directly impacts how men perceive and engage with their mental health. Historically, societal norms have dictated a version of masculinity that equates emotional resilience with silence and stoicism, often at the expense of mental well-being. This section explores how shifting these perceptions to embrace vulnerability as a strength can significantly alter the landscape of mental health support for men.

At the core of this transformation is the dismantling of harmful stereotypes that associate vulnerability with weakness. By highlighting stories of men who have openly confronted their struggles, we not only challenge these misconceptions but also pave the way for a more inclusive understanding of what it means to be strong. The acknowledgment that emotional openness and seeking help are courageous acts marks a pivotal shift in societal attitudes towards male vulnerability.

Education plays a crucial role in this change, offering new perspectives on masculinity that support emotional expression and self-awareness. Initiatives aimed at young boys and adolescents are particularly impactful, as they lay the foundation for healthier coping mechanisms and interpersonal relationships in adulthood. Through workshops, campaigns, and curriculum integration focusing on emotional intelligence and mental health awareness, we can nurture a generation more comfortable with expressing vulnerability.

- Reframing vulnerability as an aspect of true strength rather than a weakness

- Implementing educational programs that promote emotional intelligence from an early age

- Celebrating public figures and role models who speak openly about their mental health challenges

The media also holds significant sway in shaping perceptions and can contribute positively by showcasing diverse representations of masculinity that include openness about emotions and struggles. When public figures share their own experiences with mental health issues, it not only humanizes them but also sends a powerful message to fans and followers that they are not alone in their battles.

In conclusion, changing the narrative around male vulnerability involves collective efforts across various sectors of society â€" from education to media representation. By fostering environments where men feel safe to express their emotions without fear of judgment or ridicule, we move closer to breaking down the barriers preventing many from seeking help. This cultural shift towards embracing vulnerability as a facet of human strength has the potential to revolutionize mental health support for men worldwide.

References:

- Brown, BrenÃ©. "Daring Greatly: How the Courage to Be Vulnerable Transforms the Way We Live, Love, Parent, and Lead." Gotham Books, 2012.

- Kimmel, Michael. "Manhood in America: A Cultural History." Oxford University Press, 2018.

- Grohl, Dave. "The Storyteller: Tales of Life and Music." Dey Street Books, 2021.- An example of a public figure discussing personal struggles and mental health.

- "The Mask You Live In." Directed by Jennifer Siebel Newsom. The Representation Project, 2015.- A documentary exploring American masculinity and its impact on mental health.

- Way, Niobe. "Deep Secrets: Boys' Friendships and the Crisis of Connection." Harvard University Press, 2013.- Examines the importance of emotional expression among boys.

3

The Science of Anxiety in Men

3.1 Biological Factors and Anxiety

The exploration of biological factors contributing to anxiety in men is crucial for a comprehensive understanding of this complex condition. This section delves into the intricate interplay between genetics, neurobiology, and physiological responses that underpin anxiety disorders. By examining these elements, we can better appreciate the multifaceted nature of anxiety and its impact on men's mental health.

Genetics plays a significant role in predisposing individuals to anxiety disorders. Research indicates that men with a family history of anxiety are at a higher risk of developing similar conditions. This genetic vulnerability can be attributed to inherited variations in genes responsible for regulating neurotransmitters such as serotonin and gamma-aminobutyric acid (GABA), both critical in managing mood and stress responses.

Neurobiological factors further elucidate the mechanisms behind anxiety in men. Studies have shown differences in brain structure and function among those with anxiety disorders. For instance, alterations in the amygdala, a region associated with emotional processing, have been observed. These changes can lead to heightened sensitivity to stress and an exaggerated fear response, hallmark features of anxiety.

Physiological responses also play a pivotal role in the manifestation of anxiety. The body's stress response system, particularly the hypothalamic-pituitary-adrenal (HPA) axis, is often dysregulated in individuals with anxiety disorders. This dysregulation can result in an overproduction of stress hormones like cortisol, leading to physical symptoms such as increased heart rate, sweating, and muscle tension that are commonly experienced during anxious episodes.

- Genetic predisposition increases susceptibility to anxiety disorders.

- Neurobiological differences impact brain regions involved in stress and emotion regulation.

- Dysregulation of the body's stress response system exacerbates physical symptoms of anxiety.

In conclusion, understanding the biological underpinnings of anxiety is essential for developing targeted interventions that address these specific aspects. Recognizing the role of genetics, neurobiology, and physiological responses not only helps demystify the experience of anxiety but also paves the way for more effective treatments tailored to men's unique needs.

3.2 Psychological Triggers for Men

The exploration of psychological triggers for anxiety in men is a critical aspect of understanding the broader spectrum of mental health issues that disproportionately affect this demographic. While biological factors lay the groundwork for susceptibility to anxiety, it's the psychological triggers that often catalyze the onset or exacerbation of symptoms in men. This section delves into the complex interplay between societal expectations, personal identity, and stressors unique to men's experiences that contribute to their mental health challenges.

Societal expectations play a significant role in shaping how men perceive and respond to stressors. The traditional masculine ideal, which emphasizes stoicism, self-reliance, and emotional restraint, can discourage men from acknowledging feelings of anxiety or seeking help. This pressure to conform to a certain archetype of masculinity can lead to an internalization of stress and avoidance behaviors, exacerbating anxiety symptoms.

Personal identity and self-perception are also crucial factors in understanding psychological triggers for anxiety in men. Issues related to career success, financial stability, and fulfilling perceived roles as providers or protectors can significantly impact a man's self-esteem and sense of worth. The fear of failure or not living up to these expectations can trigger intense feelings of anxiety and inadequacy.

- Societal pressures to adhere to traditional masculine norms may suppress emotional expression.

- Career and financial responsibilities heavily influence men's self-perception and stress levels.

- Relationship dynamics and changes in family structure can serve as significant sources of stress.

In addition to societal pressures and personal identity concerns, specific life events such as changes in relationship status, parenting challenges, or job loss are potent triggers for anxiety. These events can challenge a man's sense of stability and control over his life, leading to increased vulnerability to anxiety disorders. Furthermore, the reluctance among many men to discuss these issues openly or seek professional help compounds the problem by delaying diagnosis and treatment.

In conclusion, understanding the psychological triggers for anxiety in men requires a nuanced approach that considers both individual vulnerabilities and broader societal influences. By recognizing these triggers, mental health professionals can develop more effective strategies tailored specifically towards men's needs, encouraging early intervention and reducing the stigma associated with seeking help for mental health issues.

3.3 The Role of Environment and Lifestyle

The environment and lifestyle choices play a pivotal role in the mental health of men, influencing the onset, severity, and management of anxiety disorders. This section delves into how external factors such as work stress, social isolation, physical activity levels, and substance use contribute to anxiety in men. Understanding these elements offers insights into preventive measures and lifestyle modifications that can mitigate anxiety symptoms.

Workplace stress is a significant environmental factor contributing to anxiety. High-pressure jobs, long working hours, job insecurity, and conflicts with colleagues or superiors can trigger or exacerbate anxiety symptoms. The competitive nature of many male-dominated industries reinforces the notion that showing vulnerability is a sign of weakness, further discouraging men from seeking help or adopting coping strategies.

Social connectionsâ€"or the lack thereofâ€"also significantly impact men's mental health. Social isolation has been linked to increased levels of anxiety and depression. Men are less likely than women to have strong social support networks due to societal expectations that discourage emotional openness among men. This lack of support can lead to feelings of loneliness and isolation, increasing susceptibility to anxiety.

Lifestyle factors such as physical activity and substance use play crucial roles in managing or triggering anxiety. Regular exercise has been shown to reduce symptoms of anxiety through the release of endorphins and improvement in overall physical health. Conversely, substance abuse—including alcohol, nicotine, and recreational drugs—can significantly worsen anxiety symptoms over time. Substance use may initially serve as a coping mechanism for stress or anxiety but ultimately leads to increased dependency and potentially more severe mental health issues.

- Work-related stressors are major contributors to male anxiety.

- Social isolation exacerbates feelings of anxiousness due to limited emotional support networks.

- Physical activity serves as an effective tool for reducing anxiety while substance abuse worsens it.

In conclusion, the interplay between environment, lifestyle choices, and mental health cannot be overstated when addressing anxiety in men. By recognizing these factors' influence on well-being, individuals can make informed decisions about their lifestyles while policymakers can create supportive environments that promote mental health awareness and encourage healthy living practices among men.

References:

- World Health Organization. (2020). Mental health and substance use. https://www.who.int/teams/mental-health-and-substance-use

- American Psychological Association. (2019). Stress in America: Stress and Current Events. https://www.apa.org/news/press/releases/stress/2019/stress-america-2019.pdf

- National Institute of Mental Health. (2021). Men and Mental Health. https://www.nimh.nih.gov/health/topics/men-and-mental-health

- Centers for Disease Control and Prevention. (2021). Anxiety and Depression in Adults: United States, 2019.https://www.cdc.gov/nchs/products/databriefs/db 377.htm

- Mental Health Foundation. (2020). Physical activity and mental health. https://www.mentalhealth.org.uk/a-to-z/p/physical-activity-and-mental-health

4

Cognitive-Behavioral Techniques for Managing Anxiety

4.1 Understanding Cognitive Distortions

The concept of cognitive distortions is pivotal in the realm of cognitive-behavioral therapy (CBT) and plays a crucial role in understanding and managing anxiety, especially within the context of adult men. Cognitive distortions are essentially irrational or exaggerated thought patterns that can contribute to heightened anxiety, depression, and a general sense of unease. Recognizing these patterns is the first step towards challenging and altering them to foster healthier thinking habits.

In "Anxiety in Adult Men: Anxiety In Men Survival Guide," the exploration of cognitive distortions serves as a foundational element for readers to grasp how their thoughts can warp their perception of reality, often leading to unnecessary stress and anxiety. This section delves deeper into common types of cognitive distortions that men may experience, providing insights into why acknowledging these patterns is essential for mental wellness.

- All-or-Nothing Thinking: This distortion involves seeing things in black-and-white categories. If one's performance falls short of perfect, he may see himself as a total failure.

- Overgeneralization: Here, an individual makes broad interpretations from a single event. For instance, if something goes wrong once, he might expect it to go wrong every time thereafter.

- Mental Filtering: This involves picking out a single negative detail and dwelling on it exclusively, thus perceiving the whole situation as negative.

- Disqualifying the Positive: Positive experiences are dismissed as flukes or not real, which maintains a negative belief despite evidence to the contrary.

- Catastrophizing: Expecting disaster to strike, no matter what. This is also known as "worst-case scenario" thinking.

Beyond identifying these distortions, "Anxiety in Adult Men" emphasizes practical strategies for challenging and reframing such thoughts. Techniques such as evidence-based questioning (asking oneself what evidence exists that supports or refutes this thought), reattribution (identifying external factors that may have contributed to an event), and scaling (putting problems into perspective) are discussed as methods to combat cognitive distortions.

This deeper understanding encourages men dealing with anxiety to recognize how their thoughts influence their feelings and behaviors. By learning to identify and adjust these distorted thought patterns through CBT techniques and mindfulness practices outlined in the book, individuals can begin to see significant improvements in their mental health outcomes. Ultimately, this section underscores the importance of self-awareness in managing anxiety and fostering resilience against stressors commonly faced by men in today's society.

4.2 Developing Coping Strategies

The progression from understanding cognitive distortions to actively developing coping strategies is a critical journey in managing anxiety, particularly for adult men who may face unique societal pressures and expectations. This section delves into the practical application of cognitive-behavioral techniques that empower individuals to constructively respond to anxiety-inducing situations. By building a toolkit of coping strategies, men can navigate their experiences with greater resilience and flexibility.

Coping strategies in the context of cognitive-behavioral therapy (CBT) are diverse, encompassing both cognitive and behavioral approaches. These strategies are designed not only to combat the immediate symptoms of anxiety but also to lay a foundation for long-term mental health and well-being. The development of these strategies involves several key steps, each tailored to address the specific nuances of an individual's experience with anxiety.

- Identifying Triggers: The first step involves recognizing the situations, thoughts, or feelings that trigger anxiety. This awareness enables individuals to prepare and apply coping strategies proactively.

- Challenging Negative Thoughts: Building on the understanding of cognitive distortions, this strategy focuses on questioning and reframing negative thought patterns into more balanced and realistic perspectives.

- Mindfulness and Relaxation Techniques: Practices such as deep breathing exercises, progressive muscle relaxation, and mindfulness meditation can help reduce physiological symptoms of anxiety by promoting relaxation and present-moment awareness.

- Problem-Solving Skills: Developing effective problem-solving skills encourages a proactive approach to dealing with stressors, focusing on finding solutions rather than dwelling on problems.

- Building Support Networks: Cultivating strong relationships with friends, family, or support groups provides emotional support and encouragement, which is vital for resilience against anxiety.

Incorporating these coping strategies into daily life requires practice and patience. It often involves trial and error to find what works best for an individual's unique circumstances. However, over time, these techniques can significantly diminish the impact of anxiety on one's life. Moreover, they foster a sense of empowerment by equipping individuals with tools to manage their mental health proactively.

This exploration into developing coping strategies underscores their importance in not just managing but thriving in the face of anxiety. By adopting a holistic approach that includes both cognitive restructuring and practical behavioral interventions, men dealing with anxiety can achieve improved mental health outcomes. Ultimately, these coping strategies serve as essential components in the journey towards resilience, well-being, and fulfillment.

4.3 Implementing Behavioral Changes

The journey from recognizing the need for change to actualizing behavioral adjustments in one's life is a pivotal phase in managing anxiety, especially after developing coping strategies. This section delves into the practical aspects of implementing these changes, focusing on how individuals can translate their cognitive and emotional insights into concrete actions that mitigate anxiety's impact. The transition from theory to practice is often where the most significant transformation occurs, marking a critical step towards sustained mental health improvement.

Implementing behavioral changes requires a structured approach that includes setting realistic goals, creating actionable plans, and employing self-monitoring techniques to track progress. This process is inherently personal and varies widely among individuals, reflecting the unique nature of each person's experience with anxiety.

- Setting Realistic Goals: The first step involves establishing clear, achievable objectives that are directly related to reducing anxiety. These goals should be specific, measurable, attainable, relevant, and time-bound (SMART). For instance, someone might aim to reduce panic attacks from three times a week to once a week within a month by applying relaxation techniques learned during therapy sessions.

- Action Plans: With goals in place, the next step is to develop detailed action plans that outline the steps needed to achieve these objectives. This might include scheduling daily mindfulness exercises, identifying and preparing for potential triggers in advance, or practicing assertive communication in relationships that typically cause stress.

- Self-Monitoring: Keeping track of one's progress is crucial for maintaining motivation and adjusting strategies as needed. Techniques such as journaling or using apps designed for mental health tracking can provide valuable insights into patterns of anxiety and the effectiveness of different coping strategies over time.

- Seeking Feedback: Regularly reviewing progress with a therapist or support group can offer additional perspectives on one's journey and help refine approaches based on feedback. It also reinforces the importance of accountability in making lasting changes.

The implementation of behavioral changes does not occur overnight but rather evolves through consistent effort and adaptation. Challenges and setbacks are an integral part of this process; however, they also present opportunities for learning and growth. By embracing these principles and persistently applying them in daily life, individuals can significantly enhance their ability to manage anxiety effectively. Ultimately, this proactive stance empowers people not just to cope with their condition but also to lead more fulfilling lives despite it.

This exploration into implementing behavioral changes underscores its significance as both an extension and application of previously developed coping strategies. It highlights how theoretical knowledge gained from cognitive-behavioral therapy must be actively applied through behavior modification techniques for genuine progress in overcoming anxiety.

References:

- American Psychological Association. (n.d.). Strategies to manage anxiety and stress. Retrieved from https://www.apa.org/topics/anxiety/stress-management

- Mayo Clinic Staff. (2021). Anxiety disorders: Treatment and therapy. Retrieved from https://www.mayoclinic.org/diseases-conditions/anxiety/diagnosis-treatment/drc-20350967

- National Health Service (NHS). (2019). Self-help therapies. Retrieved from https://www.nhs.uk/conditions/stress-anxiety-depression/self-help-therapies/

- Mind UK. (2020). How to cope with panic attacks. Retrieved from https://www.mind.org.uk/information-support/types-of-mental-health-problems/anxiety-and-panic-attacks/panic-attacks/

- Anxiety and Depression Association of America (ADAA). (n.d.). Tips to Manage Anxiety and Stress. Retrieved from https://adaa.org/tips

5

Mindfulness and Relaxation Practices

5.1 Introduction to Mindfulness

Mindfulness, a practice rooted in ancient traditions, has found its place in modern therapeutic settings as a powerful tool for enhancing mental health and well-being. At its core, mindfulness involves paying attention to the present moment with an attitude of openness, curiosity, and non-judgment. This introductory section delves into the significance of mindfulness within the context of anxiety management for adult men, highlighting how it serves as a foundational element in navigating the complexities of anxiety disorders.

The relevance of mindfulness in addressing anxiety cannot be overstated. For many men grappling with anxiety, the societal expectation to remain stoic and suppress emotional struggles can exacerbate feelings of isolation and distress. Mindfulness offers an alternative path by encouraging individuals to engage with their experiences directly and compassionately. This approach fosters a deeper understanding of one's thoughts and emotions, enabling men to break free from the cycles of avoidance and rumination that often fuel anxiety.

Integrating mindfulness into daily life begins with simple practices such as mindful breathing or body scans. These techniques anchor individuals in the present moment, reducing the tendency to get caught up in worries about the future or regrets about the past. Over time, regular mindfulness practice can significantly lower levels of stress and anxiety, improve concentration, and enhance overall quality of life.

- Developing awareness of breath as a tool for grounding oneself in moments of distress.

- Learning to observe thoughts without judgment, recognizing them as transient mental events rather than absolute truths.

- Cultivating self-compassion to counteract harsh self-criticism often associated with anxiety.

In addition to personal practice, mindfulness-based interventions such as Mindfulness-Based Stress Reduction (MBSR) or Mindfulness-Based Cognitive Therapy (MBCT) have been shown to be effective in treating anxiety disorders. These structured programs combine mindfulness techniques with elements of cognitive therapy to help individuals change their relationship with anxiety-provoking thoughts and feelings.

Ultimately, embracing mindfulness is about more than just managing symptoms; it's about enriching one's life experience and fostering resilience against future challenges. By learning to live more mindfully, men can transform their relationship with anxietyâ€"viewing it not as a weakness but as an opportunity for growth and self-discovery.

5.2 Breathing Techniques and Meditation

The practice of breathing techniques and meditation forms a cornerstone in the edifice of mindfulness, serving as both a gateway and a foundational skill for those seeking to enhance their mental well-being. This section delves into the nuanced interplay between breath control and meditative practices, elucidating how these tools can be harnessed to foster tranquility, focus, and a profound sense of presence. The relevance of these practices extends beyond mere relaxation; they are instrumental in cultivating an environment within which individuals can confront and navigate the complexities of their internal landscapes with grace and resilience.

Breathing techniques, or pranayama in the yogic tradition, offer a tangible method through which one can regulate the nervous system, thereby influencing both emotional states and physiological responses. By learning to consciously modulate breath patternsâ€"slowing down the inhalation and exhalation processesâ€"one can activate the body's parasympathetic nervous system. This activation is crucial for mitigating stress responses, reducing anxiety levels, and promoting a state of calmness that permeates both mind and body. Examples include diaphragmatic breathing, alternate nostril breathing, and paced respiration exercises.

Meditation complements breathing techniques by providing a structured framework for engaging with the present moment. Through various forms such as mindfulness meditation, loving-kindness meditation (Metta), or focused attention meditation, individuals learn to anchor their awareness in the now. This practice cultivates an observational stance towards thoughts and emotions, allowing them to pass without attachment or aversion. The act of returning one's focus to the breath or chosen object of meditation serves as a powerful exercise in mental discipline, enhancing cognitive flexibility and emotional regulation over time.

- Exploring different breathing techniques to find one that resonates personally.

- Incorporating short meditation sessions into daily routines to build consistency.

- Using guided meditations as an accessible entry point for beginners.

The synergy between breathing techniques and meditation offers a holistic approach to managing stress and anxiety. Regular practice not only improves respiratory efficiency but also deepens self-awareness and fosters an inner sanctuary of peace amidst life's tumultuous currents. As individuals become more adept at navigating their inner worlds through these practices, they unlock new dimensions of mental clarity, emotional balance, and overall well-being.

5.3 Progressive Muscle Relaxation

Progressive Muscle Relaxation (PMR) is a deep relaxation technique that has been effectively used to control stress and anxiety, relieve insomnia, and reduce symptoms of certain types of chronic pain. Developed by Dr. Edmund Jacobson in the early 20th century, this practice involves sequentially tensing and then relaxing specific muscle groups throughout the body. This process not only promotes physical relaxation but also enhances mental tranquility by shifting focus away from stressors towards bodily sensations.

The essence of PMR lies in its simplicity and the direct feedback mechanism it provides between muscular tension and relaxation. By intentionally contracting muscles before relaxing them, individuals can develop a more acute awareness of physical sensations, which often leads to greater overall relaxation. The technique starts with muscles in one area of the body—typically the feet or hands—and progressively works through other areas, culminating with the muscles of the face.

One of the key benefits of PMR is its versatility. It can be practiced almost anywhere and does not require any special equipment or extensive training to begin. Sessions can last anywhere from 5 to 20 minutes, making it an accessible tool for those with busy schedules or for individuals seeking a quick method to de-stress.

- Starting with lower extremities like toes and feet allows participants to gradually work their way up through the body, ensuring no muscle group is overlooked.

- Focusing on one muscle group at a time helps isolate tension areas, making it easier to address specific discomforts or imbalances.

- Incorporating deep breathing into PMR sessions enhances relaxation effects by promoting oxygen flow and further reducing physiological stress responses.

Research supports PMR's efficacy in improving sleep quality, suggesting that regular practice before bedtime can facilitate an easier transition into sleep. Additionally, athletes have found PMR beneficial for both pre-competition anxiety reduction and post-competition recovery by aiding in muscle recuperation.

In conclusion, Progressive Muscle Relaxation stands as a testament to the power of mind-body interventions in managing stress and enhancing well-being. Its straightforward approach empowers individuals to actively engage in their own relaxation process, fostering both immediate relief and long-term resilience against stress.

References:

- Jacobson, E. (1938). Progressive Relaxation. Chicago: University of Chicago Press.

- Conrad, A., & Roth, W.T. (2007). Muscle relaxation therapy for anxiety disorders: It works but how? Journal of Anxiety Disorders, 21(3), 243-264.

- Vickers, A., Zollman, C., & Payne, D.K. (2001). Hypnosis and relaxation therapies. Western Journal of Medicine, 175(4), 269-272.

- Manzoni, G.M., Pagnini, F., Castelnuovo, G., & Molinari, E. (2008). Relaxation training for anxiety: a ten-years systematic review with meta-analysis. BMC Psychiatry, 8(41).

6

Lifestyle Adjustments for Reducing Anxiety

6.1 Diet, Exercise, and Sleep Hygiene

The interplay between diet, exercise, and sleep hygiene forms a foundational triad in managing anxiety among adult men. This section delves into how these lifestyle adjustments can significantly mitigate symptoms of anxiety, offering practical advice for those seeking to enhance their mental health through everyday choices.

Dietary Considerations: The connection between what we eat and how we feel cannot be overstated. Nutritional psychiatry has emerged as a promising area highlighting the impact of dietary patterns on mental health. For men battling anxiety, incorporating foods rich in omega-3 fatty acids (such as salmon and flaxseeds), magnesium (found in leafy greens and nuts), and antioxidants (berries and dark chocolate) can offer mood-stabilizing benefits. Conversely, reducing intake of processed foods, caffeine, and sugar is crucial as these can exacerbate anxiety symptoms.

- Increase consumption of whole foods to stabilize blood sugar levels.

- Integrate probiotics to support gut health, which is linked to mood regulation.

- Maintain hydration as dehydration can lead to heightened stress levels.

Exercise as a Tool for Anxiety Management: Regular physical activity is a powerful antidote to anxiety. It not only diverts the mind from stressors but also enhances the body's ability to handle stress by improving resilience over time. Activities such as jogging, cycling, swimming, or even brisk walking can elevate endorphin levels, fostering a sense of well-being. Establishing a consistent exercise routine encourages discipline and provides structure, further aiding in anxiety reduction.

- Aim for at least 30 minutes of moderate exercise most days of the week.

- Incorporate strength training to build physical resilience alongside mental fortitude.

- Explore mindfulness-based exercises like yoga or tai chi that promote mental clarity.

   Sleep Hygiene Practices: Quality sleep is essential for emotional regulation and stress management. Poor sleep patterns can exacerbate feelings of anxiety; thus, establishing good sleep hygiene is critical. This includes maintaining a regular sleep schedule, creating a restful environment free from electronic distractions before bedtime, and engaging in relaxing activities such as reading or taking a warm bath prior to sleep.

- Avoid stimulants such as caffeine and nicotine close to bedtime.

- Limit exposure to screens at least an hour before going to bed to reduce blue light interference with circadian rhythms.

- Create a pre-sleep ritual that signals your body it's time to wind down.

   In conclusion, integrating mindful dietary choices with regular physical activity and disciplined sleep habits can profoundly influence one's ability to manage anxiety. These lifestyle adjustments not only improve overall well-being but also empower men dealing with anxiety by providing them with actionable strategies that foster resilience against stressors encountered in daily life.

6.2 Time Management and Work-Life Balance

The concept of time management and achieving a healthy work-life balance is crucial in the context of reducing anxiety. This section explores how effectively organizing one's time and prioritizing activities can lead to a more balanced lifestyle, thereby mitigating stress and anxiety levels. The importance of this balance cannot be overstated, as it directly impacts mental health and overall well-being.

Effective time management starts with setting clear, achievable goals and understanding the difference between urgent and important tasks. This distinction helps in prioritizing activities that contribute to long-term benefits over those that demand immediate attention but offer little value in the long run. Techniques such as the Eisenhower Box can be instrumental in categorizing tasks, thus aiding in better decision-making regarding where to allocate time and resources.

- Identify tasks that are important for your well-being and prioritize them.

- Learn to say no to demands that do not align with your priorities or contribute to your goals.

- Delegate tasks when possible to avoid taking on more than you can handle.

Achieving work-life balance requires a conscious effort to delineate boundaries between professional responsibilities and personal life. In today's digital age, where work often spills into personal time via emails and messages, setting clear boundaries is more important than ever. This might involve specific hours dedicated to work-related communications or designating certain areas at home as work-free zones.

- Establish strict start and end times for work-related activities each day.

- Incorporate breaks throughout the day to rest and recharge, avoiding burnout.

- Prioritize leisure activities that relax and rejuvenate you outside of work hours.

In conclusion, mastering time management techniques allows for a structured approach towards daily activities, ensuring that both personal well-being and professional responsibilities receive adequate attention. Simultaneously, establishing a healthy work-life balance is essential for reducing anxiety by preventing overwork and ensuring sufficient downtime for relaxation. Together, these strategies form a comprehensive approach towards managing anxiety through lifestyle adjustments focused on organization and prioritization.

6.3 Hobbies, Interests, and Social Engagement

The pursuit of hobbies, cultivation of interests, and active social engagement play pivotal roles in the holistic approach to reducing anxiety. Engaging in activities that one finds enjoyable or fulfilling can serve as a powerful counterbalance to stress, offering both psychological relief and physical benefits. This section delves into how these leisure pursuits contribute to a well-rounded lifestyle that supports mental health.

Hobbies and interests provide a valuable outlet for self-expression and creativity, which are essential for mental well-being. Whether it's painting, gardening, playing a musical instrument, or any other activity that sparks joy and interest, dedicating time to such pursuits can significantly lower stress levels. These activities offer an escape from the routine pressures of daily life, allowing individuals to focus on tasks that bring them satisfaction and a sense of accomplishment.

- Engage in activities that promote relaxation and mindfulness, such as yoga or meditation.

- Explore new hobbies that challenge you intellectually or creatively to foster personal growth.

- Set aside regular time each week for your hobbies to ensure they are a consistent part of your life.

Social engagement is equally important in managing anxiety. Building and maintaining relationships with friends, family members, or community groups provides emotional support and reduces feelings of isolation. Participating in group activities related to one's interests not only enhances social skills but also offers opportunities for positive interactions that can boost one's mood and outlook on life.

- Join clubs or groups that align with your interests to meet like-minded individuals.

- Volunteer for causes you care about to connect with others while contributing positively to your community.

- Attend workshops or classes related to your hobbies to learn new skills in a social setting.

In conclusion, integrating hobbies, interests, and social activities into one's lifestyle is crucial for mitigating anxiety. These elements encourage living in the moment and appreciating the joys found in everyday experiences. By fostering connections with others through shared interests and dedicating time to personal passions, individuals can build resilience against stress while enriching their lives with meaningful engagement.

References:

- Scott, E. (2021). "The Importance of Hobbies for Stress Relief." Verywell Mind.

- Pritchard, A. (2019). "Connecting Through Shared Interests." Psychology Today.

- Gomez, E. (2020). "Why Social Connections Make Us Happier." Harvard Business Review.

- Kabat-Zinn, J. (2018). "Wherever You Go, There You Are: Mindfulness Meditation in Everyday Life." Hyperion.

- Brown, B. (2012). "Daring Greatly: How the Courage to Be Vulnerable Transforms the Way We Live, Love, Parent, and Lead." Gotham Books.

7

Building Supportive Relationships

7.1 Cultivating Emotional Intelligence

The journey towards overcoming anxiety, especially in men, is significantly enhanced by cultivating emotional intelligence (EI). This process involves recognizing, understanding, and managing one's own emotions while also being attuned to the emotions of others. In the context of "Anxiety in Adult Men," developing EI is not just a strategy for personal growth but a critical tool for navigating the complexities of mental health challenges.

At its core, emotional intelligence comprises several key components: self-awareness, self-regulation, motivation, empathy, and social skills. Each of these plays a vital role in how individuals confront and manage anxiety. For instance, self-awareness allows men to recognize their feelings of anxiety and understand what triggers these emotions. This recognition is the first step toward addressing the root causes rather than merely coping with symptoms.

Cultivating emotional intelligence does not happen overnight; it requires consistent practice and reflection. However, the benefits extend far beyond managing anxiety alone. Improved EI can lead to better relationships, enhanced work performance, and an overall higher quality of life. By prioritizing emotional intelligence development, men can transform their approach to mental health challenges into opportunities for profound personal growth.

In conclusion, "Anxiety in Adult Men" emphasizes that cultivating emotional intelligence is not merely an adjunct to traditional anxiety management strategies but a foundational aspect of building resilience against mental health struggles. Through enhancing self-awareness, regulating emotions effectively, fostering motivation from within, practicing empathy, and honing social skills, men can navigate the path toward recovery with greater confidence and support.

- Self-Regulation: This involves controlling or redirecting disruptive emotions and impulses. Techniques such as mindfulness meditation can aid in this process by helping men observe their thoughts and feelings without judgment.

- Motivation: A high level of EI includes being able to motivate oneself to persist in face of obstacles or setbacks. For men dealing with anxiety, finding intrinsic motivationsâ€"such as personal growth or well-beingâ€"can be more effective than external rewards.

- Empathy: Understanding and sharing the feelings of others can help build supportive relationships that are crucial for mental health recovery. Empathy fosters deeper connections and provides a sense of belonging that combats isolation.

- Social Skills: Effective communication and interpersonal skills enable individuals to express their needs and boundaries clearly while also respecting those of others. These skills are essential for building trust within relationships that encourage open discussions about mental health.

7.2 Communicating About Mental Health in Relationships

Communicating about mental health within relationships is a pivotal aspect of building and maintaining supportive connections. It involves more than just sharing one's own experiences or struggles; it requires active listening, empathy, and an openness to understanding the mental health challenges faced by others. This communication fosters a deeper connection between individuals, creating a safe space where vulnerabilities can be shared without fear of judgment.

The importance of discussing mental health openly in relationships cannot be overstated. It breaks down the stigma associated with mental health issues, making it easier for individuals to seek help and support when needed. Moreover, it equips partners with the knowledge and understanding necessary to provide appropriate support during challenging times.

- Creating a Safe Space: Initiating conversations about mental health should be done in a safe and private setting, where both parties feel comfortable and secure. This encourages honesty and vulnerability.

- Using "I" Statements: When discussing personal feelings or experiences related to mental health, using "I" statements helps in expressing oneself clearly without placing blame or causing defensiveness in the other person.

- Active Listening: Being an active listener means giving full attention to the speaker, acknowledging their feelings, and responding thoughtfully. It validates the speaker's emotions and shows genuine care and concern.

- Educating Each Other: Sharing information about specific mental health conditions can help both parties understand each other's experiences better. Education fosters empathy and patience within the relationship.

Beyond individual efforts, seeking professional guidance together can also be beneficial. Couples therapy or counseling provides a structured environment for addressing mental health concerns within the context of the relationship. Professionals can offer strategies tailored to improve communication skills specifically around sensitive topics like mental health.

In conclusion, effective communication about mental health in relationships is essential for fostering strong, empathetic connections that can withstand the challenges posed by these issues. By prioritizing open dialogue, practicing active listening, and seeking mutual understanding through education and professional support, couples can create a resilient foundation that supports both individuals' mental well-being.

7.3 Creating a Support Network

The creation of a support network is an essential step in fostering resilience and well-being, particularly when navigating the complexities of mental health. This process extends beyond the confines of individual relationships to encompass a broader community of friends, family members, colleagues, and mental health professionals. A well-structured support network offers diverse perspectives and resources, ensuring that individuals have access to emotional and practical support tailored to their unique needs.

Building such a network requires intentional effort and strategy. It begins with identifying potential members who demonstrate empathy, understanding, and a willingness to engage in open dialogue about mental health issues. These individuals may come from various aspects of oneâ€™s life but share a common commitment to providing support without judgment.

- Expanding Beyond Close Relationships: While close friends and family are often core components of oneâ€™s support network, expanding this circle to include peers, mentors, or members of support groups can provide additional layers of understanding and experience.

- Leveraging Community Resources: Many communities offer resources such as workshops, seminars, or group therapy sessions focused on mental health topics. Engaging with these resources can not only broaden oneâ€™s support network but also enhance collective knowledge and coping strategies.

- Incorporating Professional Support: Mental health professionals play a crucial role in any support network. They offer expert guidance and can help navigate the challenges associated with mental health conditions. Establishing a relationship with therapists or counselors should be considered an integral part of building one's support system.

The digital age has also introduced new avenues for creating supportive connections through online forums, social media groups, and other virtual platforms dedicated to mental health discussions. These spaces can offer anonymity and accessibility for those seeking advice or sharing experiences related to their mental health journey.

In conclusion, creating a robust support network is a dynamic process that evolves according to individual needs over time. It involves both giving and receiving support in various formsâ€"emotional encouragement during difficult times, sharing informative resources for better understanding mental health issues, or simply offering companionship through shared experiences. By cultivating such networks intentionally, individuals can ensure they have access to comprehensive support systems that bolster their mental well-being.

References:

- American Psychological Association. (n.d.). Building your support network. Retrieved from https://www.apa.org

- Mental Health Foundation. (2019). How to support mental health at work. Retrieved from https://www.mentalhealth.org.uk

- National Alliance on Mental Illness. (n.d.). Find Support. Retrieved from https://www.nami.org

- Substance Abuse and Mental Health Services Administration. (SAMHSA). (n.d.). Behavioral Health Treatment Services Locator. Retrieved from https://findtreatment.samhsa.gov

- Mind for better mental health. (n.d.). Peer support. Retrieved from https://www.mind.org.uk

8

Professional Help and Therapies

8.1 Recognizing When to Seek Professional Help

The journey towards understanding and managing anxiety, especially in adult men, often involves recognizing when it is time to seek professional help. This critical step is emphasized in "Anxiety in Adult Men: Anxiety In Men Survival Guide," which aims to dismantle the barriers preventing men from addressing their mental health issues. Acknowledging the need for professional intervention can be a pivotal moment in one's path to recovery, yet many struggle with this decision due to societal expectations and personal apprehensions.

Identifying the signs that indicate a need for professional assistance is essential. These signs may include persistent feelings of worry or fear that interfere with daily activities, physical symptoms of anxiety such as restlessness or fatigue, and changes in behavior like withdrawal from social interactions or decreased performance at work. Additionally, if traditional coping mechanisms or self-help strategies fail to alleviate these symptoms, it might be time to consider seeking help from a mental health professional.

Overcoming the stigma associated with mental health care is another significant challenge addressed in the guide. Many men fear judgment or perceive seeking help as a sign of weakness due to cultural stereotypes that valorize stoicism and self-reliance. The book emphasizes the importance of changing these perceptions by highlighting stories of resilience and recovery, demonstrating that seeking help is not only an act of courage but also a crucial step towards healing.

- Understanding the difference between normal stress and anxiety disorders

- Recognizing physical symptoms that accompany psychological distress

- Acknowledging how untreated anxiety can impact relationships, work, and overall quality of life

The decision to seek professional help is deeply personal but understanding these key indicators can provide clarity and encourage individuals to take action. "Anxiety in Adult Men" serves as a comprehensive resource for those contemplating this step, offering guidance on finding qualified professionals who specialize in male mental health issues. It underscores the message that reaching out for support is a strength, not a weakness, paving the way for more open discussions about men's mental health.

8.2 Types of Therapy for Anxiety Disorders

The exploration of therapy types for anxiety disorders is crucial in understanding the broad spectrum of interventions available to individuals seeking relief from this condition. This section delves into various therapeutic approaches, highlighting their unique contributions to managing and treating anxiety disorders. The aim is to provide a comprehensive overview that not only informs but also empowers individuals in making informed decisions about their mental health care.

Anxiety disorders encompass a range of conditions, each with its own set of symptoms and challenges. Consequently, the therapeutic approach must be tailored to meet the specific needs of the individual. Among the most effective therapies are Cognitive Behavioral Therapy (CBT), Exposure Therapy, Acceptance and Commitment Therapy (ACT), and medication-assisted therapies. Each modality offers distinct mechanisms for addressing the cognitive, behavioral, and emotional aspects of anxiety.

- Cognitive Behavioral Therapy (CBT): CBT stands at the forefront of anxiety disorder treatment. It operates on the premise that negative thought patterns and beliefs significantly contribute to the development and perpetuation of anxiety. Through CBT, individuals learn to identify, challenge, and replace these maladaptive thoughts with more realistic and positive ones, thereby reducing anxious feelings.

- Exposure Therapy: This therapy is particularly beneficial for phobias and other anxiety disorders where avoidance behavior is prominent. Exposure therapy gently encourages individuals to face their fears in a controlled environment, gradually desensitizing them to the source of their anxiety over time.

- Acceptance and Commitment Therapy (ACT): ACT combines traditional behavior therapy techniques with mindfulness strategies. It teaches individuals to accept their thoughts without judgment and commit to actions that align with their values, fostering greater psychological flexibility.

- Medication-Assisted Therapies: While not a standalone solution for everyone, medications can play a critical role in managing symptoms for some individuals. They are often used in conjunction with psychotherapy to provide comprehensive treatment.

In addition to these primary therapies, innovative approaches such as Mindfulness-Based Stress Reduction (MBSR) and Dialectical Behavior Therapy (DBT) have shown promise in treating anxiety disorders by emphasizing mindfulness practices and emotional regulation skills respectively. The choice of therapy ultimately depends on individual preferences, symptom severity, and specific disorder characteristics.

The landscape of therapeutic options for anxiety disorders is rich and varied, offering hope and pathways toward recovery for those affected. By understanding the nuances of each therapy type, individuals can collaborate more effectively with healthcare providers to devise a treatment plan that addresses their unique needs.

8.3 Finding the Right Mental Health Professional

Finding the right mental health professional is a pivotal step in addressing and managing anxiety disorders effectively. This process involves understanding the different roles within mental health care, recognizing one's own needs, and navigating the healthcare system to find a suitable match. The journey to finding the right professional can significantly influence an individual's path to recovery and overall well-being.

The first step in this journey is identifying the type of mental health professional that aligns with oneâ€™s specific needs. Psychiatrists, for instance, are medical doctors who can prescribe medication and are often consulted when there is a need for pharmacological intervention alongside therapy. Psychologists, on the other hand, specialize in psychotherapy and other therapeutic interventions without prescribing medication. Licensed Clinical Social Workers (LCSWs) and Licensed Professional Counselors (LPCs) also provide therapy but might have different areas of expertise such as family counseling or substance abuse.

Understanding one's own preferences and needs is crucial in this process. Some individuals may prioritize a therapist's expertise in certain therapeutic approaches like Cognitive Behavioral Therapy (CBT) or Acceptance and Commitment Therapy (ACT), while others might value a professional's experience with specific demographics or issues such as LGBTQ+ matters, trauma, or cultural sensitivity.

- Researching potential therapists' backgrounds, qualifications, and areas of specialization can aid in making an informed decision.

- Consulting with primary care physicians or trusted healthcare providers for referrals can also lead to finding reputable professionals.

- Utilizing online directories and mental health organizations’ resources can streamline the search process.

Once potential candidates are identified, reaching out for initial consultations can provide insights into their therapeutic style and whether it aligns with one’s expectations. Many professionals offer brief initial consultations free of charge to discuss their approach and answer any questions.

Finding the right mental health professional is not always immediate and may require meeting with several therapists before finding a good fit. It’s important for individuals to trust their instincts about whether they feel comfortable and understood by their therapist. A strong therapeutic relationship is foundational to effective treatment; hence compatibility should be given significant consideration during this selection process.

In conclusion, while navigating through options may seem daunting at first, taking informed steps towards selecting a mental health professional can greatly enhance the effectiveness of therapy received. By prioritizing personal needs, conducting thorough research, and engaging in open communication during preliminary meetings, individuals can establish a beneficial partnership with their chosen therapistâ€"setting the stage for meaningful progress in managing anxiety disorders.

References:

- American Psychological Association. (n.d.). How to choose a psychologist. Retrieved from https://www.apa.org/topics/therapy/choose-psychologist

- National Alliance on Mental Illness. (n.d.). Finding a mental health professional. Retrieved from https://www.nami.org/Your-Journey/Individuals-with-Mental-Illness/Finding-a-Mental-Health-Professional

- Substance Abuse and Mental Health Services Administration. (n.d.). Behavioral Health Treatment Services Locator. Retrieved from https://findtreatment.samhsa.gov/

- Anxiety and Depression Association of America. (n.d.). Therapist Directory. Retrieved from https://adaa.org/find-help/treatment-help/therapist-directory

9

Tools for Self-Help

9.1 Mood Tracking and Journaling

Mood tracking and journaling emerge as pivotal tools in the realm of self-help, especially for men grappling with anxiety. This technique not only aids in recognizing patterns and triggers in oneâ€™s emotional landscape but also serves as a therapeutic outlet for expressing thoughts and feelings that might be difficult to articulate verbally. In the context of "Anxiety in Adult Men," mood tracking and journaling are underscored as essential practices for fostering self-awareness and facilitating recovery.

The act of mood tracking involves regularly recording one's emotional states, which can reveal insights into how various activities, interactions, and external circumstances influence oneâ€™s mental health. By maintaining a mood diary, individuals can identify specific factors that exacerbate or alleviate their anxiety, enabling them to make informed decisions about lifestyle adjustments or coping strategies. This process demystifies the often unpredictable nature of anxiety by providing tangible data that can be analyzed over time.

Journaling complements mood tracking by offering a space for deeper reflection on the emotions logged daily. It encourages individuals to explore the root causes of their feelings, examine their thought patterns, and challenge any negative beliefs that may be contributing to their anxiety. Writing about experiences and emotions can also have a cathartic effect, helping to release pent-up stress and providing a sense of relief.

Incorporating mood tracking and journaling into daily routines requires minimal resources yet yields significant benefits for mental health. These practices empower men to take an active role in managing their anxiety by developing greater self-awareness and resilience. Moreover, they serve as a reminder that personal growth is possible even amidst challenges, reinforcing the message of hope central to "Anxiety in Adult Men."

- Identification of Triggers: Through consistent mood tracking, men can pinpoint specific events or situations that trigger anxious responses.

- Behavioral Patterns: Journal entries can reveal recurring thought patterns or behaviors that either hinder or promote well-being.

- Coping Mechanisms: Reflecting on past journal entries allows individuals to recognize which coping strategies have been most effective for managing anxiety.

9.2 Utilizing Apps and Online Resources

In the digital age, leveraging apps and online resources has become a cornerstone for individuals seeking self-help methods, particularly for those dealing with anxiety. This approach complements traditional mood tracking and journaling by providing innovative tools that can be accessed anytime and anywhere, thus offering a level of convenience and immediacy not always available through other means. The significance of these digital aids lies in their ability to offer personalized experiences that cater to the unique needs of each user, making them an invaluable asset in the journey towards mental wellness.

Apps designed for mood tracking and mental health improvement use sophisticated algorithms to analyze users' input on their emotional states, activities, and thought patterns. These platforms often incorporate elements of Cognitive Behavioral Therapy (CBT), mindfulness, and stress reduction techniques, presenting them in an engaging format that encourages regular use. By doing so, they help users identify triggers more efficiently than traditional journaling might allow, thanks to real-time data collection and analysis.

Online resources extend beyond apps to include forums, educational websites, and video-based therapy sessions. These platforms provide a wealth of information on coping strategies, offer support from communities facing similar challenges, and sometimes give access to professional advice at reduced costs or even for free. The anonymity of seeking help online can also reduce the stigma associated with mental health issues, encouraging more men to take the first steps towards recovery.

- Personalized Support: Many apps offer customization options that tailor the experience to individual preferences and needs.

- Accessibility: With smartphone ownership nearly ubiquitous, these tools are readily accessible to a vast audience.

- Anonymity: Online platforms can provide a sense of privacy that encourages openness and honesty.

The integration of apps and online resources into daily routines represents a shift towards proactive self-care in mental health management. By harnessing the power of technology, individuals are empowered with immediate access to support mechanisms that can guide them through moments of anxiety. Moreover, these digital solutions stand as testament to the evolving landscape of mental health careâ€"where innovation meets accessibilityâ€"offering hope and practical assistance at the touch of a button or click of a mouse.

9.3 Worksheets for Identifying Triggers

The utilization of worksheets for identifying triggers represents a pivotal step in the self-help journey, especially for individuals grappling with emotional or psychological challenges such as anxiety, depression, or stress. These tools serve not only as a means to uncover the specific conditions or events that precipitate distress but also as a foundation for developing personalized strategies to manage and mitigate their impact. This section delves into the significance of these worksheets and explores how they can be effectively employed to enhance self-awareness and foster resilience.

Worksheets designed to identify triggers typically guide users through a process of reflection and documentation, encouraging them to record instances where negative emotions arise. This practice is rooted in the principles of Cognitive Behavioral Therapy (CBT), which posits that understanding the link between thoughts, feelings, and behaviors is crucial for emotional regulation. By systematically noting down triggering events along with the resultant thoughts and feelings, individuals can begin to discern patterns in their reactions to certain stimuli.

- Structured Reflection: Worksheets provide a structured format that prompts users to consider various aspects of their experiences, including situational context, emotional intensity, and physical sensations. This comprehensive approach ensures no critical detail is overlooked.

- Pattern Recognition: Regular use of these tools facilitates the recognition of recurring themes or conditions that act as triggers. Identifying these patterns is essential for developing targeted coping mechanisms.

- Personalized Coping Strategies: With a clear understanding of their triggers, individuals can work on crafting personalized strategies that address their unique needs and vulnerabilities. Worksheets often include sections for planning proactive responses to anticipated triggers.

In addition to fostering self-awareness, worksheets for identifying triggers also empower users by involving them actively in their own healing process.

The act of writing itself can be therapeutic, providing an outlet for expressing difficult emotions and reducing their intensity. Moreover, these worksheets can serve as valuable communication tools during therapy sessions, offering concrete examples of triggers and reactions that can be explored further with a professional.

Ultimately, worksheets for identifying triggers are more than just simple documents; they are dynamic tools that evolve with the user's journey towards mental wellness. As individuals gain deeper insights into their emotional responses and refine their coping strategies accordingly, these worksheets become tangible records of personal growth and resilience-building efforts.

References:

- Cognitive Behavioral Therapy: Techniques for Retraining Your Brain by Jason M. Satterfield (2015) - A comprehensive guide to CBT, offering insights into how identifying triggers is crucial for emotional regulation.

- The Anxiety and Phobia Workbook by Edmund J. Bourne (2020) - Provides practical exercises, including worksheets for identifying triggers, to help manage anxiety and phobias effectively.

- Mind Over Mood, Second Edition: Change How You Feel by Changing the Way You Think by Dennis Greenberger and Christine A. Padesky (2015) - Introduces techniques and worksheets designed to identify and respond to triggers in a constructive manner.

- Feeling Good: The New Mood Therapy by David D. Burns (2008) - Offers strategies for recognizing and altering negative thought patterns that trigger emotional distress.

10

Beyond Survival - Thriving with Anxiety

10.1 Reframing Anxiety as an Opportunity for Growth

The concept of reframing anxiety into an opportunity for growth is a transformative approach that shifts the narrative surrounding mental health, especially in the context of adult men. This perspective does not diminish the real and often intense experiences of anxiety but instead encourages individuals to harness these challenges as catalysts for personal development and resilience building. Understanding this reframing process is crucial for anyone looking to navigate their anxiety with a sense of purpose and empowerment.

Anxiety, traditionally seen as a hindrance, can actually serve as a powerful motivator for self-improvement and change. When men begin to view their struggles through this lens, they unlock a new realm of possibilities for coping and thriving. This shift in perception enables individuals to identify and leverage their inner strengths, learn new skills, and build confidence in their ability to manage life's uncertainties.

One key aspect of transforming anxiety into an opportunity involves embracing vulnerability. By acknowledging their fears and anxieties openly, men can break down societal stigmas that equate emotional openness with weakness. This act of courage fosters deeper connections with others, enhancing social support networks that are essential for mental well-being.

- Developing Emotional Intelligence: Recognizing and understanding one's emotions lays the groundwork for managing anxiety more effectively.

- Cultivating Mindfulness: Engaging in mindfulness practices helps individuals stay present and reduce rumination on past or future worries.

- Adopting a Growth Mindset: Viewing challenges as opportunities to learn rather than insurmountable obstacles can transform how men cope with anxiety.

Incorporating these strategies not only aids in managing symptoms but also contributes to overall personal growth. Men who reframe their experience with anxiety often report increased resilience, improved relationships, and a greater sense of fulfillment in life. Ultimately, viewing anxiety through the lens of growth empowers men to lead richer, more meaningful lives despite the challenges they face.

This approach aligns closely with the broader themes presented in "Anxiety in Adult Men: Anxiety In Men Survival Guide," emphasizing resilience, personal growth, and the breaking down of harmful stereotypes. By adopting this perspective, men can embark on a journey that not only addresses their immediate struggles with anxiety but also leads them towards becoming more rounded, emotionally intelligent individuals capable of facing life's adversities with strength and grace.

10.2 Stories of Transformation and Success

The journey from battling anxiety to thriving in spite of it is both personal and profound. The stories of transformation and success that emerge from this struggle are not just narratives of overcoming but are testaments to the human spirit's resilience. These accounts provide invaluable insights into the practical application of reframing anxiety as a growth opportunity, showcasing real-life examples of individuals who have turned their battles with anxiety into avenues for substantial personal development.

One compelling narrative involves a young entrepreneur who viewed his intense social anxiety not as a barrier but as a catalyst for mastering digital communication. His journey underscores the importance of leveraging one's unique challenges in ways that align with personal strengths and professional aspirations. By channeling his efforts into online marketing, he not only circumvented the immediate stressors associated with face-to-face interactions but also built a successful digital business platform that reached millions.

Another story features an artist who used her anxiety as a source of creative inspiration. Her art became a medium through which she could express her inner turmoil, transforming her feelings of fear and uncertainty into powerful visual statements that resonated with many. This process not only facilitated her own healing but also helped others feel seen and understood, illustrating how shared vulnerabilities can foster deep connections.

- Embracing Vulnerability: Opening up about struggles can lead to stronger relationships and community support.

- Leveraging Personal Strengths: Identifying and using one's unique abilities as tools for managing anxiety.

- Finding Creative Outlets: Using artistic expression or other hobbies as methods for coping and communicating emotions.

These stories highlight the transformative power of adopting a growth mindset towards anxiety. Individuals who have successfully navigated this path often speak of an increased sense of self-awareness, improved emotional intelligence, and enhanced life satisfaction. Their journeys illuminate the potential within all to not only survive but thrive in the face of mental health challenges by viewing them through a lens of opportunity rather than obstacle.

In essence, these narratives serve as beacons for others still navigating their way through the fog of anxiety, offering hope and demonstrating that with the right perspective and strategies, it is possible to lead a fulfilling life despite ongoing battles with anxiety. They underscore the message that while anxiety may be part of one's life, it does not define one's entirety nor limit one's capacity for success and happiness.

10.3 Maintaining Wellness Long-Term

Maintaining wellness over the long term is a critical aspect of thriving with anxiety. This journey involves not just overcoming immediate challenges but embedding practices into daily life that sustain mental health and well-being. The essence of long-term wellness lies in the continuous application of strategies learned through personal experiences of managing anxiety, as well as adopting new habits that promote emotional resilience.

One fundamental approach to sustaining wellness is through the development of a personalized self-care routine. This routine can include regular physical activity, which has been shown to reduce symptoms of anxiety and depression by releasing endorphins and improving overall physical health. Additionally, incorporating mindfulness practices such as meditation or yoga can enhance one's ability to remain present and grounded, reducing feelings of stress and worry.

Nutrition also plays a crucial role in managing anxiety over the long haul. A balanced diet rich in fruits, vegetables, whole grains, lean protein, and omega-3 fatty acids can support brain health and influence mood regulation. Conversely, reducing intake of caffeine, sugar, and processed foods can help minimize spikes in anxiety levels.

- Establishing a Support System: Building strong relationships with friends, family, or support groups provides a network of understanding and encouragement that is invaluable for long-term mental health maintenance.

- Continuous Learning: Staying informed about new research or techniques for managing anxiety encourages adaptability and growth in one’s wellness journey.

- Setting Realistic Goals: Creating achievable objectives related to personal development or wellness can foster a sense of accomplishment and progress.

Beyond individual practices, seeking professional guidance when necessary remains an essential component of maintaining long-term wellness. Regular check-ins with mental health professionals can offer fresh perspectives on coping strategies while providing support for navigating life’s ups and downs. Furthermore, engaging in cognitive-behavioral therapy (CBT) or other forms of therapy can equip individuals with tools to challenge negative thought patterns and behaviors contributing to their anxiety.

In conclusion, maintaining wellness long-term requires a multifaceted approach that includes self-care routines tailored to individual needs, nutritional considerations, building supportive relationships, continuous learning about mental health management strategies, setting realistic goals for personal growth, and seeking professional guidance when needed. By integrating these elements into daily life, individuals living with anxiety can not only manage their symptoms but thrive amidst them.

References:

- Mayo Clinic Staff. (2021). Anxiety disorders. Mayo Clinic. Retrieved from https://www.mayoclinic.org/diseases-conditions/anxiety/symptoms-causes/syc-20350961

- National Institute of Mental Health. (2021). Anxiety Disorders. NIMH. Retrieved from https://www.nimh.nih.gov/health/topics/anxiety-disorders

- American Psychological Association. (n.d.). How to manage stress and anxiety. APA. Retrieved from https://www.apa.org/topics/stress-anxiety-relief

- Harvard Health Publishing. (2020). The gut-brain connection. Harvard Medical School. Retrieved from https://www.health.harvard.edu/diseases-and-conditions/the-gut-brain-connection

- Mental Health Foundation. (2019). Physical activity and mental health. Retrieved from https://www.mentalhealth.org.uk/a-to-z/p/physical-activity-and-mental-health

11

Additional Resources

11.1 Recommended Reading List

The "Anxiety in Adult Men: Anxiety In Men Survival Guide" stands out as a pivotal resource for understanding and navigating the complexities of anxiety disorders in men. However, to deepen one's comprehension and toolkit for dealing with anxiety, a curated reading list can provide additional perspectives and strategies. This selection encompasses a range of topics from understanding the psychological underpinnings of anxiety to practical self-help guides that complement the foundational knowledge provided by "Anxiety in Adult Men". Each book has been chosen for its potential to enrich the reader's journey towards wellness.

This recommended reading list serves as an extension of the conversation started by "Anxiety in

Adult Men", offering varied approaches to mental health challenges faced by men today. Whether you're looking for scientific insights into the nature of trauma and anxiety or practical guides on managing your mental health day-to-day, these books provide valuable resources on your path toward healing.

- "The Body Keeps the Score: Brain, Mind, and Body in the Healing of Trauma" by Bessel van der Kolk - This book delves into how trauma reshapes both body and brain, compromising sufferers' capacities for pleasure, engagement, self-control, and trust. It offers a new understanding of the impacts of trauma and pathways to recovery.

- "Feeling Good: The New Mood Therapy" by David D. Burns - A seminal work in the field of cognitive therapy, this book provides powerful tools for individuals dealing with depression, anxiety, and other mood disorders. Its techniques are based on principles that readers can apply independently or alongside professional treatment.

- "Dare: The New Way to End Anxiety and Stop Panic Attacks" by Barry McDonagh - Focusing on overcoming panic attacks and reducing general anxiety through unique strategies that differ from traditional therapy or medication routes. Itâ€™s particularly useful for those seeking immediate coping mechanisms.

- "Mind Over Mood: Change How You Feel by Changing the Way You Think" by Dennis Greenberger and Christine A. Padesky - This workbook offers a hands-on approach to improving emotional health through cognitive behavioral therapy (CBT) techniques. It's especially beneficial for readers who appreciate structured exercises and actionable advice.

- "No More Mr Nice Guy: A Proven Plan for Getting What You Want in Love, Sex, and Life" by Robert A. Glover - While not exclusively about anxiety, this book addresses patterns of behavior that many men find themselves trapped in which can contribute to feelings of frustration and indirectly to anxiety.

11.2 Helpful Websites and Apps

In the digital age, accessing resources to manage and understand anxiety has become more straightforward, thanks to a plethora of websites and apps designed with mental health in mind. These platforms offer a range of tools from guided meditations to cognitive behavioral therapy (CBT) exercises, making support both accessible and varied to suit individual needs. This section delves into some of the most impactful websites and apps that have been recognized for their contributions to mental wellness.

One standout website is **Anxiety.org**. It serves as a comprehensive resource for those seeking information on all types of anxiety disorders. The site combines research-based information with practical advice, offering articles, treatment options, and personal stories that provide both insight and comfort to individuals facing anxiety. Its holistic approach ensures users can find not just definitions and symptoms but also coping strategies and community support.

When it comes to apps, **Headspace** has emerged as a leader in mindfulness and meditation. Designed to help users reduce stress and improve their overall mental health, Headspace offers guided meditations, sleep sounds, and breathing exercises. Its user-friendly interface makes it easy for beginners to start meditating, while its diverse range of content keeps long-term users engaged.

- Calm - Another popular app that focuses on reducing anxiety through meditation, sleep stories, and music designed to soothe the mind.

- Moodfit - A customizable app that allows users to track their mood, understand what affects it, and provides actionable insights into improving mental health.

- Talkspace - An online therapy platform that connects users with licensed therapists for text-based counseling sessions, making professional help accessible without having to leave home.

Beyond these examples lies a vast ecosystem of digital tools aimed at supporting mental health. From forums like *7 Cups*, which offers free emotional support from trained volunteers, to specialized apps like *Dare*, which helps users confront panic attacks through exposure therapy techniques; the digital landscape is rich with opportunities for learning about managing anxiety. While these resources do not replace professional medical advice or treatment when needed, they provide valuable support for those looking to manage their day-to-day mental health.

In conclusion, the proliferation of helpful websites and apps has significantly contributed to breaking down barriers around mental health care by providing immediate access to support tools. Whether someone is seeking knowledge about their condition or looking for daily practices to alleviate stress and anxiety symptoms, there's likely a digital solution available that can meet their needs.

11.3 Locating Support Groups

Finding the right support group can be a pivotal step in managing and overcoming anxiety. While digital tools offer immediate and accessible options, the value of human connection through support groups cannot be overstated. These groups provide a safe space for sharing experiences, learning coping strategies, and feeling understood by others facing similar challenges. This section explores various avenues to locate such support groups, expanding on the digital landscape into more traditional yet equally impactful resources.

Community centers often serve as hubs for various support groups, including those focused on mental health and anxiety. By visiting or contacting local community centers, individuals can inquire about scheduled meetings or resources that lead to finding a suitable group. Libraries, another cornerstone of community resources, frequently host or have information on support group meetings. Bulletin boards in these spaces often carry notices about upcoming gatherings.

Hospitals and clinics are also instrumental in connecting individuals with support groups. Many healthcare providers recognize the therapeutic benefits of peer support in conjunction with medical treatment for anxiety disorders. As such, they may facilitate groups directly or refer patients to external ones that align with their needs.

- Mental health organizations and charities often maintain directories of support groups on their websites. Organizations like the National Alliance on Mental Illness (NAMI) provide extensive lists and contacts for local chapters offering group support.

- Online platforms specifically designed for mental health support play a crucial role in bridging distances between individuals seeking help. Websites like Meetup.com allow users to search for or create meetups around mental health topics, including anxiety.

- Social media networks have given rise to numerous private groups where members share their experiences and advice regarding anxiety management. These platforms offer an easily accessible way to connect with peers globally.

In conclusion, locating a supportive community is more accessible than ever before thanks to a blend of traditional methods and modern technology. Whether through face-to-face meetings facilitated by community centers and healthcare providers or virtual connections made via social media and specialized online platforms, there is a plethora of options available for anyone seeking solidarity in their journey towards mental wellness.

References:

- National Alliance on Mental Illness (NAMI) - https://www.nami.org: Offers extensive resources and a directory for local support groups focusing on mental health, including anxiety.

- Meetup.com - https://www.meetup.com: A platform that allows users to find or create meetups around various topics, including mental health and anxiety support groups.

- Mental Health America (MHA) - https://www.mhanational.org: Provides information on finding support groups and other resources for those dealing with anxiety and other mental health issues.

12

Embracing Change and Growth

12.1 Accepting Change as a Constant in Life

Understanding and accepting change as an inevitable part of life is crucial, especially for individuals grappling with anxiety. This concept is particularly relevant when considering the unique challenges faced by men in acknowledging and addressing their mental health issues. The societal expectation for men to embody strength and stoicism can often exacerbate feelings of anxiety, making the acceptance of change even more daunting.

The journey towards accepting change begins with recognizing that life's only constant is change itself. This realization can be both liberating and intimidating. For men dealing with anxiety, acknowledging that change is inevitable can serve as the first step towards managing their condition more effectively. It encourages a shift in perspective—from viewing change as a threat to seeing it as an opportunity for growth and self-discovery.

One of the key strategies for embracing change involves developing resilience. Resilience allows individuals to adapt to new circumstances, challenges, and environments with greater ease. It involves cultivating a mindset that views obstacles not as insurmountable barriers but as chances to learn and evolve. Building resilience can be particularly empowering for men who have been conditioned to suppress their vulnerabilities.

- Practicing mindfulness and staying present can help manage the fear of the unknown associated with change.

- Seeking support from friends, family, or mental health professionals can provide a safe space to express concerns and navigate through periods of transition.

- Engaging in regular physical activity has been shown to reduce symptoms of anxiety and improve overall well-being, making it easier to cope with changes.

Incorporating these practices into daily life does not eliminate the challenges posed by change but equips individuals with tools to approach them more constructively. By fostering an environment where vulnerability is not seen as weakness but as part of being human, men can begin to view their journey through anxiety not just as a path towards managing symptoms but also as an opportunity for profound personal transformation.

In conclusion, accepting change as a constant requires a multifaceted approach that includes changing perceptions about masculinity and mental health, building resilience, seeking support, and practicing self-care. Through this comprehensive approach, "Anxiety in Adult Men: Anxiety In Men Survival Guide" aims not only to address the symptoms of anxiety but also to empower readers to lead lives marked by growth, fulfillment, and acceptance of life's ever-present changes.

12.2 Navigating Transitions and Uncertainty

Navigating through transitions and uncertainty is an integral part of embracing change and growth. This phase often involves stepping into the unknown, which can be a source of anxiety and fear for many individuals, especially men who are conditioned to maintain a facade of strength in the face of adversity. The journey through transitions and uncertainty requires not just acceptance but also active engagement with one's inner self and the external environment.

The first step in navigating these challenging times is acknowledging the presence of uncertainty as a natural aspect of life's dynamics. It's about understanding that uncertainty isn't necessarily an obstacle but rather a pathway to new opportunities and learning experiences. This perspective shift is crucial for developing resilience, enabling individuals to remain flexible and open-minded during periods of change.

- Creating a personal vision or goal can serve as a guiding light during uncertain times, providing direction and purpose.

- Establishing routines or practices that foster emotional stability and physical well-being can help maintain balance amidst change.

- Embracing community support, whether through friends, family, or professional networks, offers reassurance and practical advice when facing new challenges.

In addition to these strategies, it's important to cultivate patience and compassion towards oneself during transitional phases. Self-compassion encourages a kinder internal dialogue, which is particularly beneficial when confronting failure or setbacks. Moreover, engaging in reflective practices such as journaling or meditation can enhance self-awareness, allowing individuals to process their emotions more effectively and make informed decisions aligned with their core values.

Ultimately, navigating transitions and uncertainty is about harnessing inner strengths while remaining open to external support. It involves a delicate balance between planning for the future and staying present in the momentâ€"acknowledging fears but not being defined by them. By adopting this multifaceted approach, individuals can move through periods of change with greater confidence and emerge stronger on the other side.

This exploration underscores the importance of viewing transitions not just as periods to endure but as opportunities for profound personal growth. Through proactive engagement with both internal responses and external resources, navigating through uncertainty becomes less daunting and more empowering.

12.3 Cultivating Resilience and Adaptability

The journey of cultivating resilience and adaptability is a cornerstone in navigating life's inevitable changes and uncertainties. This process involves more than merely surviving; it's about thriving amidst challenges, learning to pivot when necessary, and growing stronger through adversity. Resilience is the inner strength that helps individuals bounce back from setbacks, while adaptability allows them to adjust their course of action based on new circumstances or information.

One key aspect of building resilience is developing a positive mindset. This doesn't mean ignoring difficulties or pretending everything is fine when it isn't. Instead, it's about maintaining a hopeful outlook, focusing on solutions rather than problems, and viewing challenges as opportunities for growth. A positive mindset encourages perseverance and can significantly impact one’s ability to recover from stress or trauma.

- Practicing mindfulness and stress-reduction techniques can enhance emotional regulation, an essential component of resilience. Techniques such as deep breathing, meditation, or yoga help maintain calmness and clarity in the face of adversity.

- Building a strong support network is crucial for resilience. Knowing there are people who care and will offer support makes facing challenges less daunting.

- Adaptability requires a willingness to learn from experiences and an openness to change. It involves being flexible with plans and expectations, which can lead to discovering new paths that may not have been considered before.

To further cultivate adaptability, individuals should embrace lifelong learning—seeking out new knowledge, skills, and experiences that enrich their understanding of the world and themselves. This continuous growth mindset ensures that one remains relevant and capable of adjusting to change effectively.

In conclusion, cultivating resilience and adaptability is not a passive process but an active engagement with lifeâ€™s complexities. It requires introspection, effort, and the courage to face fears head-on. By fostering these qualities within themselves, individuals not only navigate transitions more smoothly but also emerge from them enriched by the experience. The path towards resilience and adaptability is both challenging and rewarding; it shapes character, builds depth of spirit, and ultimately leads to a more fulfilling life.

References:

- American Psychological Association. (n.d.). Building your resilience. https://www.apa.org/topics/resilience

- Mindful. (2021). How to Practice Mindfulness. https://www.mindful.org/how-to-practice-mindfulness/

- PositivePsychology.com. (2021). 27 Resilience Activities and Worksheets for Students and Adults (+PDFs). https://positivepsychology.com/resilience-activities-worksheets/

- Verywell Mind. (2022). What Is Adaptability? https://www.verywellmind.com/what-is-adaptability-5120674

- Harvard Business Review. (2011). Learning to Live with Complexity. https://hbr.org/2011/09/learning-to-live-with-complexity

"Anxiety in Adult Men: Anxiety In Men Survival Guide" is a pioneering non-fiction work that addresses the critical yet often neglected issue of anxiety disorders among men. This book stands out for its comprehensive approach to understanding and managing anxiety, specifically tailored to the unique challenges faced by men. It aims to dismantle societal stigmas surrounding male vulnerability and provides a plethora of practical strategies for overcoming anxiety.

The guide begins with an exploration of anxiety disorders, detailing their symptoms, causes, and how they can manifest differently in men compared to women. It highlights the societal pressures that discourage men from seeking help and offers solutions for navigating these barriers. Central to the book is its focus on actionable tools for managing anxiety, including cognitive-behavioral techniques, mindfulness practices, lifestyle adjustments, and advice on when professional intervention is necessary.

Furthermore, the importance of supportive relationships and emotional intelligence in recovery is emphasized, advocating for open discussions about mental health in various social settings. The narrative also celebrates resilience and personal growth, viewing anxiety not as a flaw but as an opportunity for self-improvement. Inspirational stories from men who have successfully dealt with their anxiety are interspersed throughout.

Additionally, "Anxiety in Adult Men" serves as a resource hub offering worksheets, app recommendations, further reading suggestions, and tips for finding specialized mental health professionals. This book not only educates but also empowers readers to transform their relationship with anxiety and regain control over their lives. It marks a significant step towards changing societal perceptions of male vulnerability and mental health.

www.ingramcontent.com/pod-product-compliance
Lightning Source LLC
Chambersburg PA
CBHW071038250726
48653CB00005B/1886